SUCCESS
AGAINST
ALL ODDS

Printed in the United Kingdom in March 2017
by T. Snape & Co., Ltd., Preston. Tel: 01772 254553
© 2017 Lekan Wellington Adegunwa
ISBN 9780995789302

Cover Design by David Akinwusi (DavoGraph Studio)

Contact Details
+44 (0) 7738 738155
www.lekanadegunwa.com
www.trmchurch.org
www.facebook.com/pastorlekan
lekanadegunwa@hotmail.com

DEDICATION

This book is dedicated to the reader.

I believe in your success story.

ACKNOWLEDGEMENT

My gratitude goes to the Almighty God for His abundant grace and the wisdom He has given.

I am always grateful for the beautiful family God has given to me. Thank you for your support.

One tree cannot make a forest. No one achieves greatness on their own. I want to say a big thank you to all the people who gave their time and energy to the success of this book. You are blessed.

I thank God for all the members and leaders of TRM Church for their support and prayers. It is a great privilege to serve you.

CHAPTERS

CHAPTER ONE

CREATED FOR SUCCESS

Beloved, I pray that you may prosper in all things and be in health, just as your soul prospers.

3 John 2 (NKJV)

You have suddenly discovered that there is something about you that is greater and better than where you are now. Maybe your life has been a collection of stories of averages and failures. In the midst of all these dissatisfactions, you still believe that it is not over yet, that you are still able to make a great success of your life. What you are feeling right now is not peculiar to you. You will not be able to get rid of the appetite to make something greater out of your life until you choose to actually begin to change your story. God has created each one of us with the appetite to succeed. It is abnormal for anyone to comfortably settle for a life of failure.

You will not be able to get rid of the appetite to make something greater out of your life until you choose to actually begin to change your story.

Every one of us has been created with an embedded ability and divine enablement to succeed and prosper in life. The divine desire is the success of all. There is no one who is reading this book who cannot be successful in life. The seed of success is in you. You can achieve great results in life if you dare.

Fulfilling purpose and achieving results is a lifelong process of overcoming barriers and obstacles. No one achieves much in life without having to contend with obstacles and hindrances. It is safe therefore, to define success as overcoming obstacles in life and delivering results irrespective of limitations. In the history of man, every good work we enjoy today was done by men who were able to overcome challenges and subdue obstacles and barriers. From the smallest inventions to the biggest discoveries – people have had to go beyond their limitations to deliver results that have become so beneficial to the human race. There was a time when malaria was such a deadly pestilence until it was overcome by scientific research. Polio had rendered so many people disabled until it was overcome by science. In all fields of human endeavour, achievement or success is impossible except we are ready to face challenges and overcome them. When the Wright brothers proposed that it was possible for man to fly, they seemed like lunatics to many people. Now, we fly without even thinking about it. It has now become part of our life. We are even talking about going to the moon for holidays!

God has created each one of us with the appetite to succeed. It is abnormal for anyone to comfortably settle for a life of failure.

Those who are not ready to subdue barriers should not expect to make their lives count or become what God has planned for them to become in this world. From the very beginning when God promised the seed, Jesus Christ our Lord, His conquering and purchase of salvation was wrapped up within the parameters of barriers and obstacles that He had to overcome. Most importantly, He had to break through into the flesh, be fashioned as a man and destroy the power of satan and death for mankind in order to purchase salvation for us through His sacrifice.

In the history of man, every good work we enjoy today was done by men who were able to overcome challenges and subdue obstacles and barriers.

There is so much work for us to do for the kingdom of God and for the fulfilment of our purposes and dreams but many of us seem to be held back by various experiences and limiting forces. No one will ever get to a place in life where there are no barriers to overcome in the pursuit of dreams and aspirations. Let me make it clear that facing barriers in life is not just for some; it is for everyone who aspires to make their life count. God has not called us to do anything that is impossible for us to achieve. Every God-given assignment comes with divine empowerment but we cannot operate beyond what we know and are ready to apply.

EVERYBODY CAN SUCCEED BUT NOT EVERYBODY WILL SUCCEED

Only those who are ready to pay the price, fight their fears and contend with limitations will reap the result that is called success. Success is not a destination, it is the overcoming of obstacles as we contend earnestly for our dreams and visions. How many people are ready to forge ahead in life and pursue their dreams with confidence? We are not made to fit in or stay contained. We are invincible and able by the working of God's great power in us and through us. My agenda is to introduce us to various divine mind-sets that we need to break barriers in life, exceed every limitation and cross every line that has been drawn to limit our fulfilment in life. Get ready for a life transforming experience. Get ready for a life of fulfilment and unstoppable success. You can never remain at the same level in life after reading this book. This is your season of transformation. This is your season of emergence. Your time of lack and obscurity has expired. You can begin to celebrate. The sacrifice of Jesus has made success available to you but you have to arise and be ready to lay hold of that success against all odds. You have sufficient grace to succeed and you are not going to allow the lies of the enemy stop you from a great life today.

Only those who are ready to pay the price, fight their fears and contend with barriers to overcome limitations will reap the result that is called success.

In order to be truly successful, it is very important to have a very robust understanding of what success really means. It is only after we have defined the basis for our success that we can sincerely pursue what will make us happy in life.

CHAPTER TWO

DEFINITION OF SUCCESS

For we dare not class ourselves or compare ourselves with those who commend themselves. But they, measuring themselves by themselves, and comparing themselves among themselves, are not wise.

2 Corinthians 10:12-13 (NKJV)

Just imagine! Two men who were in their late sixties were discussing what they have achieved in life. One of these men was clearly more excited to the amazement of the other person. What exactly was making him so glad? He had just one small house and a very small car, living a very basic life with his wife. This man obviously felt very successful and happy about how his life had turned out. The other man who had a fleet of cars and so many houses in different nations of the world was not that excited because he didn't feel that he had achieved so much in life. What a contradiction. You would have thought the man with so many houses and material possessions should be the happier of the two. No, it doesn't work like that. Their definition of success was different. One was satisfied just to know that he had trained his children well and that they had settled down well in life. That was what he wanted and that was what he achieved. The other man suddenly discovered after amassing so much that there were other things that were very important to him in life. He had pursued goals that did not bring him satisfaction and happiness at this stage of his life.

> *Many people have a wrong definition of success and that is one of the main reasons for many sad people in the world.*

Your definition of success is very essential to a life of happiness and significance. Many people have a wrong definition of success and that is one of the main reasons for many sad people in the world. There are so many people in life who are seeking something else apart from genuine success. They toil and labour to get what they call success only to discover a life of dissatisfaction and the insatiable desire for more. What is the use of spending a significant part of one's life to pursue a mirage? You must be very clear about what success means to you. This will allow you to face life with confidence and assurance that you are living for what will give you happiness in life.

Genuine success is not defined by what other people think about you. There are so many people that men will call successful and yet they are filled with all manner of sadness and dissatisfaction. There are people who have also allowed sadness into their own lives because of what others think about their achievements. Do not give anyone the power to determine the parameters for your success. Most times, no one can really tell that you are successful except you.

Men will fail to accurately define your success for you. You must be able to define your success for yourself.

You are the only one who knows the innermost feeling you have based on the things you have achieved. Men will fail to accurately define your success for you. You must be able to define your success for yourself.

Genuine success is not defined by material acquisition or the accumulation of wealth. Money is good and many people have loads of it but are still not happy. Money and the accumulation of material things cannot be equal to success. Success is beyond what you have and what you do not have. Real success is a function of what you are doing and what you have done. Success is not about having as much as it is about giving. Real success is about giving oneself out.

Success is not about having as much as it is about giving. Real success is about giving oneself out.

My aim is not to introduce you to what somebody else is doing. I am talking about your own personal success. We are not talking about what others are doing. We are not talking about what others want you to do. This success is not defined by the aspirations of your friends or family members. Real success is beyond all that.

Genuine success is not defined by prevailing environmental factors. Success to many people is only as defined by their environment and prevailing circumstances. If your success is defined by your environment, that means you could be successful in one country and be unsuccessful in another country. Many people therefore think changing location will make them successful. I understand that there are environmental circumstances favourable to a better delivery of result in life but we should be careful not to subject ourselves to the deception of guaranteed success based only on our environment.

PURPOSE IS THE DEFINITION OF SUCCESS.

If real success is beyond what people think or what is happening around you, then real success has to be connected to something that is inherent inside of you. There has to be another way to determine your own success without submitting to the parameters that other people have set in place around you. This inherent standard is your PURPOSE in life. This purpose is given by God and it is woven into the fabric of our existence. Knowing what we have been created to do is the beginning of our quest to genuine success. Real success is only defined by purpose. We can say with this understanding that your success is the accomplishment of your purpose. Notice that this purpose is peculiar to you and so your success must be peculiar to you.

We feel genuinely successful when we begin to enjoy the satisfaction that flows from the accomplishment of our own purpose in life.

Your purpose in life will determine what success is to you and what you should spend your time and energy pursuing. If you arrive at any other destination, you will still be unsuccessful because you have not achieved your purpose. We feel genuinely successful when we begin to enjoy the satisfaction that flows from the accomplishment of our own purpose in life.

In order to have a fulfilled life, a life which is characterised by true happiness and satisfaction, you must be clear about your dreams, your vison and your mission in life. Whatever you are hoping to achieve must be clearly understood. Many people leave their own personal vision and purpose and try to build and walk on another man's path. It never works like that. Whatever you end up achieving will not bring the satisfaction that true success brings. No one is an island, but each one of us must know what our contribution to life is, that is what will bring us true success. It is important for you to support other people's vision, but make sure whatever you do is connected to your own purpose.

COMPARATIVE SUCCESS SYNDROME

When people are sad because they feel they are not successful in comparison to others; it is a disease. I refer to this as comparative success syndrome. Many people are quick to define success by comparing themselves or others with somebody else. This appetite to compare has brought many people into anger, envy and jealousy.

When people are sad because they feel that they are not successful in comparison to others; it is a disease.

This is so pathetic because it makes people disregard their own success while they are trying hard to become somebody else. Successful people are not clones. Successful people have their own identities. They are unique. Their success is defined by their purpose in life. They will learn from others and seek support when needed but they are always true to their own purpose. When your definition of success is wrong, you end up working hard to become a clone.

> For we dare not class ourselves or compare ourselves with those who commend themselves. But they, measuring themselves by themselves, and comparing themselves among themselves, are not wise.
>
> *2 Corinthians 10:12-13 (NKJV)*

Wise people do not compare themselves with other people in order to commend themselves. Your success cannot be measured by the success of other people. Most people are not really seeking success; they just want to be better than someone else. If they cannot be better than others they spend their energy copying and struggling to show forth what others will perceive as success. This is really not the will of God for you. You cannot afford to throw away your purpose and uniqueness in order to become somebody else. It does not matter who you become, if you are not YOU, you have failed. Don't compare yourself with other people. Don't get involved in the rat race because you are not a rat. Even if you win, you are still going to be a rat. You are definitely better than that.

Successful people are not clones. Successful people have their own identities. They are unique. Their Success is defined by their purpose in life.

Focus on your purpose and spend your time and energy on your own success journey. Let your purpose be the definition of your own success. Stay away from comparative success. If their purpose is not your purpose, their success cannot be your success. You are unique and your success is unique.

SUCCESS IS A JOURNEY

We are never going to arrive at a destination called success. Success is a lifestyle. It is a continuous journey and pathway that we choose to walk every day of our lives. We shall celebrate along the pathway but we shall never get to a place where all has been done and there is nothing left for us to do. The journey of success is similar to a project. Until we have finished the project and commissioned the project, we have to continue every day of the process to work towards the achievement of our objectives. Success is a project that will last a lifetime. When we get to our milestones, we should celebrate and rejoice. We should never settle with our milestones and become conceited in ourselves.

Success is a lifestyle. It is a continuous journey and pathway that we choose to walk every day of our lives.

It is important that we are ready to persevere, fight and grow in order to maintain a life of continuous and meaningful success. You are about to get equipped with practical knowledge on how to continue in this journey of success against all odds.

CHAPTER THREE

SUCCESS AGAINST ALL ODDS

Yet in all these things we are more than conquerors through Him who loved us.

Romans 8:37 (NKJV)

Challenges are common to all men. No one will go through this world and achieve purpose without having to face challenges. These challenges often present themselves in the form of obstacles and barriers in our paths to the fulfilment of divine purpose. Many people have lived less than happy lives because they were unable to get beyond the barriers that have invaded their paths. It is important for me at this juncture to explain in details how some of these obstacles and barriers are formed in our paths and how to get victory over them.

YOUR BACKGROUND CANNOT STOP YOU

Many people are held back in life because they think their unfavourable background is a deterrent to a life of fulfilment and exploits. Sincerely, we do not have the same family or environmental backgrounds – some are more favourable than others. What is certain is that people all over the world have been able to fulfil purpose and achieve success irrespective of their backgrounds. Too many people are quick to surrender in life to whatever comes their way. Such people are always complaining about others who have been able to make it and are often deluded into thinking that those who are doing well in life are doing so just because they have privileged backgrounds. You might have an unfortunate background but your back does not have to remain on the ground. When God made you, He knew the family that you will come through to this world. Your family background can never be a tenable reason for lack of fulfilment in life.

> *You might have an unfortunate background but your back does not have to remain on the ground.*

The country you were born in or the passport you hold does not determine whether you will fulfil purpose or not. We should pursue God and not family heritage and citizenship of some so-called privileged countries. As children of God what matters is that we are citizens of heaven and that God is our Father and Jesus is our Brother and Saviour and the Holy Spirit is our Help and Guide. If you are looking for the most privileged background, don't look any further, you already have the best!

> *When God made you, He knew the family that you will come through to this world. Your family background can never be a tenable reason for lack of fulfilment in life.*

What happens to people early in life can truly shape their future. Many people have gone through experiences in early life that have badly affected the way they view life and how they respond to life challenges. What the enemy wants is to allow their past and history to hinder their tomorrow. You couldn't influence what happened to you then, you were probably powerless and unable to restrict the attack of the enemy. That was then, this is now. Do not allow the enemy to use your past against you and your beautiful destiny. You are going somewhere great and God is on your side. I know many things have happened in your life that you could do nothing about the outcome, do not lose heart. God still has the plan for your life under control. Have you been dropped by those you were entrusted to, like Mephibosheth? Mephibosheth had an unfortunate experience as recorded in the following bible passage.

> Jonathan, Saul's son, had a son who was lame in his feet. He was five years old when the news about Saul and Jonathan came from Jezreel; and his nurse took him up and fled. And it happened, as she made haste to flee, that he fell and became lame. His name was Mephibosheth.
>
> *2 Samuel 4:4 (NKJV)*

Mephibosheth had the best nurse, probably the most qualified in his day because he was a prince. It is important to know that only God can carry you and not drop you. Mephibosheth was dropped while he was a child and was lame all his life! That is not the end of the story.

You might have been dropped by someone, mistreated and abused, please, do not allow that unfortunate circumstance to rule over your life.

Jonathan his father had a covenant with David. When Jonathan died, the covenant he had with David brought Mephibosheth to the palace. We have a better covenant through the sacrifice of Jesus. It does not matter how bad things have been, God has brought you back into the palace. You have a better position in Christ than Mephibosheth had with David. You might have been dropped by someone, mistreated and abused, please, do not allow that unfortunate circumstance to rule over your life. You can choose to begin again. You can trust God for a new beginning in Christ. If you are alive to read this, I am sure that God is about to do something momentous in your life. Keep on believing, you will fulfil purpose and achieve the satisfaction of success in life.

LEARN TO LIVE YOUR LIFE

I am so glad for you because I know God's thoughts about you are greater and bigger than what any man can think of you. Many lives have been made small by words that were spoken to them. Many people have been unfortunate to listen to the wrong voices. Have you been told that you are useless and will amount to nothing? Don't ever believe them. God is saying better things about you. You are better and greater than what any man can say about you. Whether you like it or not, people around you will always have their own perceptions of your personality and what they think you can achieve in life. Sometimes their perceptions may be favourable to your growth in life but most times we meet people who are so myopic about the plans of God for our lives. They are not your God and you should never allow anyone to speak words over your life to define your boundaries for success. What men say does not matter if it contradicts what God is saying in your life. Whose report do you want to believe? God has the final say over your life. God never calls you weak, rubbish, useless or incapable. Who told you that you cannot make it in life? They have spoken against the word of God concerning you and you should disregard what they have said. It does not matter who is speaking, it does not matter how close they are to you. If anyone speaks weakness and hopelessness into your life you have every right with God to refuse, reject and discard whatever they have spoken.

Don't lose your mind over what people said against you because you need your mind to do what God wants you to do.

There are so many people walking with their heads bowed, ruminating over wicked words that faithless people have spoken into their lives. You need to pick yourself up, this is the devil's agenda to keep your life bowed as well. Don't lose your sleep over people who don't like you. Don't lose your mind over what people said against you because you need your mind to do what God wants you to do.

You need your mind to be successful in life. Don't build your life on the words of men, dwell on the word of God and this barrier will soon collapse in your life. Remember, you are beautifully and wonderfully made by God. Jesus has sacrificed so much for you that whatever happens in your life cannot change the plan of God for you. Stand up in the grace of God and be ready to live abundantly as you reign in life.

GO BEYOND THE STATUS QUO

It is needful to know that you are unique. God does not want you to fit in with people, He wants you to be yourself and fulfil your own purpose. If there is someone else who can fulfil your dreams, God wouldn't have created you. You are here for a specific purpose. You will not achieve your purpose in life by fitting in with everyone and everything around you. The world around us is full of various activities and different voices.

When the status quo and the standards set are opposed to the word and the plans of God for our lives, we should be quick to dismiss it.

There are standards set everywhere which determines what people do and how they live their lives. Most men are conformists, they always tend to agree with the status quo without questioning it. Many people have been hindered in the path of their fulfilment because they are too careful about what is happening around them. They do not want to be different. There are times when good standards are set around us which could be supportive of our dreams but we should never be carried away into making such human standards a substitute for the word of God in our lives. When the status quo and the standards set are opposed to the word and the plans of God for our lives, we should be quick to dismiss it.

The question I often ask people who are ready to follow the status quo is "who created the standard?" Most times, people don't even know, they have just been told, "this is how to do this and that is how not to do that". Many people are governed by principles that have no root in the word of God. Who said you must be a particular sex or age before you can fulfil your dream? Who said you can't buy a house now or start your own business? Who is telling you "it is never done like that"? You have to be courageous to face life the way God is leading you in order to become what God wants you to be. Break away from the status quo and live a life of freedom by the grace of God.

GO BEYOND LIMITING VIEWPOINTS

Don't be bound by world views. Don't allow the news to influence you more than your purpose and determination to succeed. Those who allow their lives to be governed by the news might not have enough time to make the news. We live in a world that is changing. A world that is always shifting its focus and response to the main issues of life. In 2009, the economy failed and the best economists and financial gurus were caught off guard. They were unable to prevent the danger or even provide a tangible and workable response to the failure of the financial market. This is not a debate about the crisis. My focus here is to emphasise that the best of the world systems and ideologies can collapse without notice. Those who are ruled by the news on CNN and SKY will have their lives governed and controlled by the things they were told. The press got it wrong about the EU referendum in the UK in 2016 and in the same year got it totally wrong about the US presidency. Be careful what you allow to run your life.

Those who allow their lives to be governed by the news might not have enough time to make the news.

One amazing fact is that so many people made more money during the financial crisis than they did before that crisis. Almost all the forecasts about housing in the UK have been very unreliable. Everyone is playing a game of chance, they have to keep reeling the stories out to be on the job. Do not be deceived, we need to overcome these barriers and give our lives a meaning.

As Christians, we should never allow world views and events to dictate the pace of our faith in God. We are not trying to deny the crisis, I am saying we can break that barrier and become what God wants us to become irrespective of the issues that are ruling the world around us. There is a saying that you might not be able to stop a bird from flying over your head but you sure can stop the bird from perching on your head. Political and economic crisis in particular have a way of demoralising many and quenching the impetus for pursuing dreams. We should not become preys, we sure can trust God to keep us in line with His will.

Remember your decisions determine your actions, your actions determine your destination.

What information forms our world view? What kind and colour of glasses are you seeing through? How you see things will affect the actions you will take; your sight is the foundation for your perception. If your sight is coloured, your perception will be coloured. If your perception is coloured your decisions will be coloured. If your decision is coloured, your actions will be coloured. Remember your decisions determine your actions, your actions determine your destination. When every other thing becomes unstable, the word of God remains the same. We are not supposed to build our lives on the government or the news, we are supposed to live by faith and not by sight. We are a people of faith. We believe in God Almighty who is always stable and faithful in all situations.

GO BEYOND PERSONAL LIMITATIONS

These limitations may be self-imposed or caused by habits that have been tolerated over time. These limitations manifest themselves in the way we see ourselves which affects what we choose to do or not do. We cannot overcome external barriers in life until we have first overcome the barriers that are innate and resident within us. For most people, it is the personal limitations that actually stop them from reaching their goals and aspirations. These are barriers that no one needs to cope with because Jesus Christ has paid all the price that is necessary for every one of us to live a life of abundance. It is essential that we make up our minds that we are not going to stop ourselves.

We cannot overcome external barriers in life until we have first overcome the barriers that are innate and resident within us.

There are people who are so pessimistic about their own capabilities. Even when others try to encourage them to pursue their dreams they always write themselves off. Some people just don't think they can do anything worthwhile in life. That is not the mind of Christ; such a mindset cannot lead to success in life. When a man operates with this kind of perception, they are always handicapped and restrained from going forward in life. These people always submit to whatever happens. They often accept a state of helplessness which saps them of any impetus or energy to make a change in their personal circumstances. We cannot overemphasise this, we should never see ourselves any less than God sees us. We are people of strength not of weakness and we should be ready to fight every form of negative perception with the word of God.

What is needful for fulfilment of dreams is more than mere education that we receive from the four walls of a classroom.

Some other people have erroneously concluded that they are not educated enough to fulfil their purpose. That is not true. There is nothing wrong with having good education but there is everything wrong with thinking that without education you cannot fulfil your dreams. By all means get education, be learned but don't ever think it is the only prerequisite for success in life. Jesus didn't just choose disciples who were educated. The bible informs us that Peter and John were unlearned! What is needful for fulfilment of dreams is more than mere education that we receive from the four walls of a classroom. We have so many examples in the world of business, religion and sports. There are so many people who have not been formally educated, they have not received any degree of any sort, but have maximised opportunities and have been able to make their lives count. Don't allow education to be your barrier. Break that barrier and move on with your life.

GO BEYOND NEGATIVE EMOTIONS

Many people are allowing themselves to be hindered in life by the "little foxes that always spoil the vine". Most times, what stops people from success is in their lives. It is not sufficient to know that good and great habits are essential for success, it is pertinent to deal with bad habits of all sorts. Do not allow negative emotions like fear and anxiety rule your life. Get rid of laziness, envy, jealousy and bitterness. You are always in a better position to succeed in life if your mind is free and your heart is pure towards yourself and other people. Before you start complaining that no one wants to give you space to express your talents and gifts, you need to ask yourself about your attitude to life.

I want to use this short story to illustrate how people sometimes struggle to move forward in life when they cannot manage negative emotions. A man was in an interview for a fantastic job that he had been trusting God for. He had prayed and fasted for many years since he lost his previous job. This man had a serious problem with controlling his anger. He would burst out in anger at every opportunity, especially when things were not going the way he preferred. As his interview progressed, one of the interviewers spilled a glass of water on the table by mistake which poured across the table onto the lap of this brother. His countenance changed - the interviewer apologised and continued with his question but the brother could not get himself out of this fallen countenance with anger written all over his face. Only God knows what he could have said if it was in a different context. All the same his anger was vivid enough and it was clear that he could not manage the situation. After a few hours on the same day, he got the result of the interview. He did well with all his answers but was not employed because they had doubts that he would be able to control his actions if offended at work. He had applied for a post that meant he would be managing a few other employees. Now, that was not really the devil, he should have controlled himself. It was not that they did not like him or that he had some bad luck, he simply, should have managed his anger appropriately. He should have known that negative emotions can bring losses in life.

> *You are always in a better position to succeed in life if your mind is free and your heart is pure towards yourself and other people.*

I don't know how far you have gone in life with bitterness, anger, envy, jealousy, pride and many more, what I am sure of is that you will struggle to make a serious impact in life for a long time if you allow these negative emotions to rule your life. You can do something about it. You can depend on God to help you. Remember, you will not be able to successfully deal with external barriers if you are full of negative emotions. These emotions will stop you more than anyone or anything can do.

DO NOT PROCRASTINATE

This is time to take action. Do something about the things that are hindering you. Please do not procrastinate. A man was tired of procrastination in his life. This habit had hindered him greatly. Now the habit was having a very bad effect on his marriage and family. When his Pastor asked him what he thought he could do, he said, "prayer will sort it out". Then the Pastor told him to pray now, but he would not. "I will pray when I get home" was his answer! He had just procrastinated the prayer. I pray that God will deliver every reader of this book from procrastination. The best time to deal with procrastination is now, prayer will help but you need some determination, ask the Holy Spirit to help you as you make up your mind to act now. Procrastination robs you of time to pursue your dreams. It gives you a false sense of abundance of time and makes you think you always have more time than everyone else. All you have is 24hrs in a day and 7 days in a week, nobody has more than 52 weeks in a year. Break that bondage, step out and do something today.

Procrastination robs you of time to pursue your dreams. It gives you a false sense of abundance of time and makes you think you always have more time than everyone else.

Maybe you have procrastinated for too long and now you feel that time is no more on your side, all you have to do is to trust God for another chance to make your life count and to do what needs to be done to get out of this position. There is always hope for everyone that is joined to the living.

CHAPTER FOUR

THE MIND OF SUCCESS

For God has not given us a spirit of fear, but of power and of love and of a sound mind.

2 Timothy 1:7 (NKJV)

The journey of success begins in the mind. It is important that the mind is well prepared and nurtured if success must be attained. An untrained mind cannot break through the limitations of life. The greatest barrier to advancement in life is a negative mind.

For the weapons of our warfare are not carnal but mighty in God for pulling down strongholds, casting down arguments and every high thing that exalts itself against the knowledge of God, bringing every thought into captivity to the obedience of Christ,

II Corinthians 10:4 – 5 (NKJV)

Whatever controls your mind controls your outcome. You must win the battle of the mind before you can deliver tangible results in life. It is our responsibility to bring our minds to a state of positive functionality and not allow our minds to be weighed down by crippling thoughts and negative ideas. Many people are caught in the quagmire of small mindedness. A lot of people are not as bound with any other thing as much as they are bound with chains in the prison cells of their minds.

Whatever controls your mind controls your outcome. You must win the battle of the mind before you can deliver tangible results in life.

The account that follows show how a majority of the leaders of Israel submitted themselves and their followers to defeat because they had a wrong mindset.

> And they gave the children of Israel a bad report of the land which they had spied out, saying, "The land through which we have gone as spies is a land that devours its inhabitants, and all the people whom we saw in it are men of great stature. There we saw the giants (the descendants of Anak came from the giants); and we were like grasshoppers in our own sight, and so we were in their sight."
>
> *Numbers 13:32-33 (NKJV)*

The children of Israel became established in Egypt so much so that even when they were cramped and limited by space, they were ready to stay there forever. In fact, when they left, it was impossible to get Egypt out of their life. You cannot go further than your mind.

A lot of people are not as bound with any other thing as much as they are bound with chains in the prison cells of their minds.

The minds of the Children of Israel stayed in Egypt. Hence, they could not advance into Canaan. Only those whose minds were free from Egypt and those who freed themselves from the memories and the slavery of Egypt were able to get into the Promised Land. If you cannot get it into your mind, you cannot get it into your life! Many people are trying in vain to get their lives and their bodies to a place their minds do not want to go. It will not work.

If you cannot get it into your mind, you cannot get it into your life!

Your mind has to get there before your body. Your body cannot limit you if your mind can find expression. Your mind is your starting point; this is where the battle begins. You cannot fight what you have submitted to.

YOUR POINT OF VIEW IS A FUNCTION OF YOUR VIEW POINT

These spies were elders but they had a small mind. Your biological age is not a true test of your mind. When someone's mind is small, every obstacle around becomes very big and overwhelming. The problem of these spies was not caused by their physical size, it was caused by a dysfunction of their mindset. Their minds were small. They came back with an evil report and caused the people to tremble.

Your view point determines what you see. How high is your view point?

When you walk through a high street with shops on both sides of the road, you will notice that most sign boards and adverts are on the first floor of the buildings. This is because no one really looks up on the high street. People keep their focus straight. On the contrary, when you drive on the highway, sign boards are generally high and above the eye level. This is because on the highway, drivers are trained to be more observant and to look way ahead of their positions. Your view point determines what you see. How high is your view point? A low view point will only see low things but a high view point will see more. If you are on the mountain top you will see more than those on the plain ground because of your view point. Your mind determines how you see what you see and determines how you interpret your data. Your point of view is a function of your view point. How you see things and what you see depends on where you stand.

YOUR VIEW POINT IS A FUNCTION OF YOUR MIND-SET

A man cannot go or grow beyond his mind. What your mind sees is where your life will go. Your mind-set dictates the direction for your life. In as much as the children of Israel saw themselves as grasshoppers, they were already defeated even before the battle commenced. They were ready to run away like grasshoppers running away from danger. Many people are so weak in their minds that the smallest of barriers causes them to tremble and to run away from their inheritance. Most times, people suffer not because they do not have the ability to succeed but because they do not have the MIND to make use of their ability. We first have to break barriers in our minds before we can break barriers in our lives.

Most times, people suffer not because they do not have the ability to succeed but because they do not have the MIND to make use of their ability.

If your mind cannot break free, how do you intend to break free from the things that are around you? How could the leaders of Israel expect to possess the land when they had defeated themselves mentally by not allowing the word of God influence their minds? Remember, Caleb and Joshua saw the same place and the same people but they were holding on to the word of God and would not allow the devil to influence their minds in order to gain advantage over them. Both of them were ready to fight to possess what God had given to them!

Your mindset will determine your success in life. If you always believe you are unable, you will struggle to generate the strength that is required to be successful.

THE "SMALL" BIG ELEPHANT

Let us learn some lessons from circus trainers. Elephants are big and yet they are comfortably controlled and tamed by their owners. Circus trainers understand that if you can conquer the mind of the elephant, you can control its massive physical size with relative ease. From infants, baby elephants are tied down to a very strong stake or tree but when the elephants become old, there is no more need for the big stake. A small one will do the job. The adult elephant, even though very powerful, intelligent and mighty, will stay bound by an insignificant stake. This is because the elephant while very young, has tried but in vain to break free from the chain of his life. After many trials and failures, the elephant accepts his fate and stops struggling to break free. Even though just a little push would have set the adult elephant free, the elephant lacks the strength of mind to try. Many people in life are bound by very fragile stakes. Even though they have enough wisdom, ability and strength to break free, they will not even try. The pain of their childhood has put their minds in a state of stupor such that they are unwilling to break free from their bondages.

Many things holding people back in life that do not allow them to pursue their dreams are nothing but a mirage.

Circus trainers understand that if you can conquer the mind of the elephant, you can control its massive physical size with relative ease.

Many Christians are like the big elephant tied down with some flimsy and powerless restraint because the enemy knows their minds are captured. The devil does not just want evil things to happen to you, he wants every evil thing to remain and rule your mind. He wants to rule your mind with bad memories. He wants the abuse, the hatred, the mistreatment, the agony and the pain you have been through in life to remain in your mind. It does not matter when you go through any bad experiences, you need to know that the devil is fighting against your future. He wants your mind in bondage, he wants you to resign from pursuing your dreams, he wants you to throw in the towel and feel sorry for yourself continuously. The devil is a liar!

> And do not be conformed to this world, but be transformed by the renewing of your mind, that you may prove what is that good and acceptable and perfect will of God.
>
> *Romans 12:2 NKJV*

Jesus paid the price for your freedom. You are completely free and empowered to excel in life. God is not just with you, God is in you. You are too powerful to relinquish your dream to the enemy. You cannot afford to be subdued by your past; move beyond that and let the word of God renew your mind.

FREE YOUR MIND

Conformity is the default position that every natural man assumes in life. People tend to become what their environment is suggesting. When they are from a poor neighbourhood, they assume the same mindset and struggle to pursue a higher dream in life. The government has tried but failed to help people from negative backgrounds to do well. In most countries in the world, there are neighbourhoods, towns and cities whose inhabitants are predictable failures. Individuals must be ready to break free and find expression for their personal purpose in life. If not, success will remain only as a topic for discussion without any significant changes in people.

Uncommon achievers and successful people believe differently and act differently in order to get a different result. We should not allow our feelings to dictate our aspirations. We should not only go for what seems available. We should push the boundaries and expand our minds. There is no limit to what we can achieve if we allow the word of God to stretch our minds. There is no success in sight for anyone who is trapped in the smallness of their mind. If you do not want to conform, you need to work on your mind, you need to free your mind. Successful people are barrier breakers. They are mindful to first break the barriers and the limitations of their minds. You need to be free and fly out of every limitation like a bird out of a cage!

Uncommon achievers and successful people believe differently and act differently in order to get a different result.

Transformation has to be deliberate and intentional. Those whose minds are bound and submissive to the elements of this world cannot exercise the freedom and the liberty that we should be experiencing in this world. There are many Christians who are living below the standards of God not because they are not gifted but because they are conforming and not renewing their minds to position themselves for transformation. Come on, you have to believe fully that Jesus paid the full price for your victory. You should not accept another day of frustration in your life. Stand up and walk into the abundance of inheritance that is yours in Christ Jesus.

You are too gifted to be suffering. When Peter was afraid of sinking, he began to sink even though he had been a professional fisherman all his life.

You are designed for success. Have you ever seen a fish afraid of drowning? Fishes don't drown in water, they are designed by God for the water. You are fashioned and packaged by God for dominion. You cannot be disadvantaged and defeated. You have the God-factor in your DNA guaranteeing success all the time! Wow! You need to be convinced of the grace of God which is sufficient for you. You are too gifted to be suffering. When Peter was afraid of sinking, he began to sink even though he had been a professional fisherman all his life. Birds are never afraid to fly, you are an eagle not an ostrich, you are made to fly higher than where you are now. You have to do something, you have to move. You have the power and the presence of the Almighty God. Your past is no longer powerful, successful people don't allow their past to subdue their present capacity.

> Therefore gird up the loins of your mind, be sober, and rest your hope fully upon the grace that is to be brought to you at the revelation of Jesus Christ; as obedient children, not conforming yourselves to the former lusts, as in your ignorance;
>
> *I Peter 1:13 – 14 (NKJV)*

Rest your hope fully on the grace of God. You have no reason to back away from your dreams.

CHAPTER FIVE
WRITE YOUR SUCCESS STORY

I can do all things through Christ who strengthens me.

Philippians 4:13 (NKJV)

When you attend a football match of say 70,000 people in attendance, only 22 players and the officials are actually doing something to influence the game. The others have only come to watch and are expected to accept whatever result is given to them after the 90 mins. To be able to influence the game, you must first be on the right bench and then be prepared to do something. Many people are full of complaints after the match but really could not have done anything about the outcome. Your life is more than a football match and you cannot follow the multitudes, you must be ready to be different in order to do what others will not do. Many people have assumed a spectator position in life, hands are folded and comments are made but nothing really important is being done to affect or change the outcome of their lives. If you are not ready to be an active player on the field of life, do not expect to make any significant changes to the outcome of your life. Talkers don't get things done. Don't follow the multitude, many people like to talk but only a few are ready to do. Be a doer.

Then David spoke to the men who stood by him, saying, "What shall be done for the man who kills this Philistine and takes away the reproach from Israel? For who is this uncircumcised Philistine, that he should defy the armies of the living God?"

I Samuel 17:26 (NKJV)

David was young and according to the recruitment standard, he was probably not experienced enough to be in the army. David dared to be different. He did not allow their mindsets about the problem to influence his decisions. He decided against the limitations imposed by the spectators. He wanted to be a real player. It is impossible to make changes in our lives that will lead to success if we do not consciously move away from talking into actually doing.

If you are not ready to be an active player on the field of life, do not expect to make any significant changes to the outcome of your life.

There is no factor of life that can hold you back if you choose to follow your purpose and move beyond limiting thoughts and ideas. David refused to queue behind people who were not ready to move forward in life. You must be careful whose lead you are following. You cannot stay behind a parked vehicle and expect to advance to your preferred destination.

Who and what defines the parameters for your life? The circumstances of life cannot put a restriction upon your life if you refuse to allow it.

DO NOT BE A PRETENDER, BE A CONTENDER

Many people are pretenders, they are not the real deal! It is not strange to have people who are running ahead and struggling to show up without a serious intent to be properly involved. If you pattern your life after them, you will soon discover as David discovered that they were only there to spectate – not to kill Goliath. When God gives you an opportunity, don't allow the enemy to restrict your thinking. David was not supposed to be there. David was not qualified to be there but he defeated Goliath! David was inspired by his passion for God to do something that others were not ready to do. Those who have gone before you are not always ahead of you.

If you are not ready to be different, do not expect to be exceptional. David was exceptional because he first dared to be different.

If you do what everyone is doing, you will achieve the result that everyone is achieving. David wanted more than them, he wanted to fulfil purpose, he wanted to do something to influence the outcome. David wanted to bring value and meaning to the whole story. He wasn't going to achieve that by being a mediocre like the rest of the people. He had to be different. If you are not ready to be different, do not expect to be exceptional. David was exceptional because he first dared to be different. He gained for himself what every other person would have loved to have – the king's daughter. You cannot secure a better tomorrow if you are not ready to break boundaries set by men and the human mind.

BE PREPARED TO FOLLOW UNPOPULAR PATH

Learn to follow an unpopular path. The road to the fulfilment of your purpose might not be a very popular one. Most times if you want to achieve what is worthwhile, operating on a lonely road might be one of the sacrifices you should be ready to make.

> When we lose the right to be different, we lose the privilege to be free.
>
> *– Charles Evans Hughes*

In the bible, Joshua chapter 6, God's preferred solution for Joshua and the children of Israel on how to bring down the walls of Jericho and win the battle was a very funny one. God wanted them to sing and walk round the massive wall in order to bring the wall down. It was absurd and nonsensical but it delivered the result when they obeyed and implemented the strategy that they were given. God's ways and strategies are not always very popular and may not be accepted but they are sure to deliver the result. Now let's be real, how difficult do you think it would be for these people who were men of war to be told to walk round the wall instead of fighting.

Sometimes we are so accustomed to the difficult way that we often consider it ridiculous to follow the simple instructions that God is giving. In the pursuit of purpose and success, we should be ready to follow the unpopular pathway. You might have an idea that seems so uncommon and new, don't discard it, stay with the idea, study it and seek to understand it very well. Many people have thrown away great ideas and strategies for increase because it did not look familiar or great at that moment.

Sometimes in life, the things you have always known may not be sufficient to bring you the desired result. We are quick to present our CVs to God but can I tell you that sometimes your CV is not enough to deliver the victory into your hands. Saul had a better CV than David in the eyes of men when they had to face Goliath but God was interested in other things, David could listen to God and do it God's way. Praise God, he got the result that others couldn't get. To become successful in life, you have to learn to walk some lonely roads. God knows what He is doing and those unpopular instructions will separate you from the crowd.

Sometimes in life, the things you have always known may not be sufficient to bring you the desired result.

In the gospel, according to Mark, chapter 2, some folks wanted to get to Jesus with their friend to receive a miracle from Him, but it was not going to be easy. "And when they could not come near Him because of the crowd, they uncovered the roof where He was. So when they had broken through, they let down the bed on which the paralytic was lying." (Mark 2:4 (NKJV)). It was difficult and almost impossible for them to gain access to Jesus. They thought of a way out. I want to assure you that there is always a way out of every limitation if only we are ready to break the barriers and open up the roof. What physical limitations are on your path, you have to start doing something about them rather than just wishing or talking about them. It is needful that you start doing something practical to move yourself against gates and doors that are shut against you and your dreams.

I want to assure you that there is always a way out of every limitation if only we are ready to break the barriers and open up the roof.

These people were determined to get through to the place of their dreams. They were not going to accept a refusal or a denial of that which they greatly desired to achieve. They didn't bow to the limitations; they didn't give in to the obstacles. They were ready to break the roof and come in through an unprecedented channel. They would not allow themselves to be held back by other people's opinions or interpretations of their actions. They were only positively driven by the dreams they had. Many of us are too careful, we are too apologetic about personal convictions. It is important that we resolve within ourselves how far we are willing to go in order to achieve result. There are limitations set everywhere in life, barrier breakers are determined to go beyond the limitations and get across the line. Many people are easily discouraged when they face obstacles. Barrier breakers are not like that. You will refuse to be discouraged if you are desperate to reach your goal. Whatever God has set before you is achievable if you are ready to get the things done irrespective of what roof might be in your way.

TAKE RESPONSIBILITY

Learn to take Responsibility. There are so many challenges in our world today. There seems to be chaos of some sort in every nation of the world. What is also very common in our global village is the fact that we have lost the sense of personal and individual responsibility. There is always somebody or some institution to blame for every predicament and problem that people face. Until personal responsibility improves in our world, we will continue to talk about various challenges – like obesity, illiteracy, teenage pregnancy, abortion, drugs and many more without any serious movement towards procuring solutions.

When we fail to take responsibility, we lose the power to effect change in our lives.

Many people might decide not to take responsibility but those who would be successful in life must have a different stand. Those who are not ready to take responsibility should not expect to take control of their destiny. You must accept responsibility before you can effect change in your life. We must begin to write our success stories by taking responsibility for our lives. When we fail to take responsibility, we lose the power to effect change in our lives. We really do not have a choice in the matter. We cannot afford to be lackadaisical about it.

In the story about David and Goliath, David achieved the success and the victory he had over Goliath because he decided to take responsibility. What Goliath demanded was for someone to accept the responsibility to take him on and David did.

David was not doing this just for himself, he wanted the whole world to know that there is a God in Israel. He could not stand the reproach, he was not going to keep quiet while Goliath defied the Holy God of Israel.

It is crucial that we all take up the challenge to move our lives forward in the pathway of success. Are you ready to make your light shine? No one will make your light shine for you. It is your responsibility and until you make it shine, no one will come to the brightness of your light. We are the planting of the Lord that He might be glorified. You cannot live an average life. You cannot run away from the battle. You have to make your life count for the glory of the Lord. Successful and exceptional people are ready to represent God, they do not seek glory but they bring glory to God and become the conveyer of His blessing and power. You are the determining factor for your tomorrow! Take responsibility for your life.

No one will make your light shine for you, it is your responsibility and until you make it shine, no one will come to the brightness of your light.

If you really want to be successful, you will be prepared to face your challenges. Those who are committed to success will not point accusing fingers at others for their own shortcomings and failures. Remember, only those who can stand up to their mistakes and challenges can get over them.

In Genesis chapter 4, verses 3 -7, two brothers, Cain and Abel brought sacrifices to God. Abel was successful with his sacrifice and the Lord having respect for him accepted his sacrifice. Cain was not that fortunate, his sacrifice needed re-presentation to secure success so that he also could be accepted. Instead of Cain to take responsibility, face the challenge and be prepared to make amends, he decided to be angry with Abel for doing well. Many people are like Cain, instead of finding ways to get result for themselves, they are busy pointing accusing fingers and trying to condemn the success of other people. It is crucial to note that the acceptance of Abel is not connected to the rejection of Cain. They were different people and their success was dependent on their peculiar purpose and what they had been designed by God to do. Cain became unduly angry and killed his brother instead of facing his problem and making amends. When people do not have something worthwhile to do, they have sufficient time to pull other people down. Do not see others as a threat.

> *When people do not have something worthwhile to do, they have sufficient time to pull other people down.*

Many people are limited in life because they are not ready to take charge and make the necessary changes that are required to move them unto success in life. You can always be better if you are ready to face your challenges. There is no need to become bitter and negative because of your present situation, seek to change what is not working and apply your energy to what will move you forward in life, you are too gifted to spend your time trying to seek the downfall of others.

ROLL AWAY THE STONE

> Jesus said, "Take away the stone." Martha, the sister of him who was dead, said to Him, "Lord, by this time there is a stench, for he has been dead four days." Jesus said to her, "Did I not say to you that if you would believe you would see the glory of God?" Then they took away the stone from the place where the dead man was lying. And Jesus lifted up His eyes and said, "Father, I thank You that You have heard Me.
>
> *John 11:39 – 41 (NKJV)*

You must be prepared to roll away the stone. There are heights you will not get to in your quest for success and significance in life if you are not ready to face the challenges and be prepared to roll away the stones. There are times that you must be ready to despise the stench and the agony of your past in order to open yourself up for a greater dimension of the power and the grace of God. If Mary and Martha had not taken away the stone, it would not have been possible for them to open the hopelessness of their situation to the release of God's power. There are so many miracles you will enjoy in life if only you are ready to put shame behind you, get rid of a pity-party mindset and do away with mourners. Do not confine your destiny to the grave, there is still a great hope for you if you are ready to be a believer of possibilities.

There are times that you must be ready to despise the stench and the agony of your past in order to open yourself up for a greater dimension of the power and the grace of God.

Don't let your past hold you bound. Even if what happened in your past was your fault, you can step away from it and move on to your next level. God is giving you a command to roll away the stone because He is prepared to do something new and spectacular in your life. Successful people will not allow the limitations of the past to hinder them from moving on in hope for a better tomorrow.

CHAPTER SIX

BECOMING UNSTOPPABLE

Looking unto Jesus, the author and finisher of our faith, who for the joy that was set before Him endured the cross, despising the shame, and has sat down at the right hand of the throne of God.

Hebrews 12:2 (NKJV)

In this chapter, I want to share with you some vital principles that will make you unstoppable in your success journey. Success is a life project; many people try very hard to begin this journey but fail to continue to a place of influence and significance. It is essential that we develop the right principles, attitudes and habits that will keep us on track. Anyone could be distracted in this journey. Losing impetus and energy for consistency is natural if we are not determined to remain on track.

BE PURPOSEFUL

So the men of Israel said, "Have you seen this man who has come up? Surely he has come up to defy Israel; and it shall be that the man who kills him the king will enrich with great riches, will give him his daughter, and give his father's house exemption from taxes in Israel." Then David spoke to the men who stood by him, saying, "What shall be done for the man who kills this Philistine and takes away the reproach from Israel? For who is this uncircumcised Philistine, that he should defy the armies of the living God?" And the people answered him in this manner, saying, "So shall it be done for the man who kills him."

I Samuel 17:25 – 27 (NKJV)

David had a clear purpose for engaging Goliath in the fight. It was not just some random and unrestrained appetite for a street fight. He knew exactly why the fight was necessary for him. You must always be clear about the purpose before you set out to pursue your goals in life. When the challenges are tough, your purpose will give you strength and keep you on track. David's purpose was clear. He wanted to take away the reproach of Goliath from Israel.

Success is a life project; many people try very hard to begin this journey but fail to continue to a place of influence and significance.

Always remember that purpose is the only true measure of success. You need to know WHY you are doing what you are doing. Successful people create focus, they have purpose and are driven to get results. They know why they are in it, they understand the demand and the goal - they know where God is taking them. David was not self-seeking, he had a clear purpose that was even beyond his personal gain. He asked the right questions and made sure that he understood what he was getting himself into even before he started.

SET YOUR EYES ON THE PRIZE

> Looking unto Jesus, the author and finisher of our faith, who for the joy that was set before Him endured the cross, despising the shame, and has sat down at the right hand of the throne of God.
>
> *Hebrews 12:2 (NKJV)*

There is no tomorrow without a target. Your target propels you, compels you and will not allow you to stop until you achieve. Those who are not goal getters are weak, confused and tired all the time. David was clear about the prize that was waiting for him. All the soldiers would have loved to marry the princess but it was not a clear goal for them so that desire did not translate into energy and strength for battle.

We need to be clear that there is reward in labour and those who are given to success are always aware that there is a prize at the end of their effort.

Jesus Christ our Saviour remained focused to achieve the highest success of procuring salvation by making sure that His eyes were set on the prize. He focused on the joy that was set before Him. We need to be clear that there is reward in labour and those who are given to success are always aware that there is a prize at the end of their effort. What exactly is keeping you motivated?

RUN INTO THE BATTLE

> So it was, when the Philistine arose and came and drew near to meet David, that David hurried and ran toward the army to meet the Philistine.
>
> *1 Samuel 17:48 (NKJV)*

Promptness is essential for continuous success in life. There is a limit to what anyone can achieve if they are slow, slothful and lackadaisical in their approach to a task. As soon as David had decided that the battle was worthwhile, he was ready to attack with speed. David ran into battle, he would not allow Goliath to dictate the pace, he was in the offensive and was ready to shoot before Goliath was set to fight. David was swift and very fast. Many people are too slow to remain successful.

Promptness is essential for continuous success in life. There is a limit to what anyone can achieve if they are slow, slothful and lackadaisical in their approach to task.

Successful people are not just interested, they are committed. They are persistent and tenacious. They will not be hindered by anything, they will not bow to intimidation. They are not lazy, they do not fold their arms waiting for things to happen.

> So the watchman reported, saying, "He went up to them and is not coming back; and the driving is like the driving of Jehu the son of Nimshi, for he drives furiously!"
>
> *2 Kings 9:20 (NKJV)*

Jehu was on a divine assignment and he considered the matter urgent. Jehu was identified just by the way he approached the battle. You must be known to be a goal getter, swift and very fast. Sometimes, the difference between failure and success is speed! Successful people make things happen. They determine the terms of reference, they do not wait for the enemy to decide what they do - they choose what to do and how to move.

START NOW

> Though your beginning was small, Yet your latter end would increase abundantly.
>
> *Job 8:7 (NKJV)*

Procrastination is dangerous; it erodes the energy required to see our decisions through to fruition. Many people are unable to pursue their dreams and overcome challenges in life because they are waiting for everything to be in place before they start. Barrier breakers are ready to start from somewhere even when that start seems low and lonely. Rome was not built in a day. Those who are not ready to start small are not ready to become big.

> For who has despised the day of small things? For these seven rejoice to see The plumb line in the hand of Zerubbabel. They are the eyes of the LORD, Which scan to and fro throughout the whole earth."
>
> *Zechariah 4:10 (NKJV)*

Waiting till everything is perfect is a barrier on its own and the only way to overcome that challenge is by doing something now.

Those who are not ready to start small are not ready to become big.

What are you still waiting for? You do not have all the time on your side, the only time you are permitted to wait is when God is saying so. When we procrastinate, we lose the desire to do. Procrastination is a barrier and the only way to overcome it is by doing it right now. Destroy that habit today by doing it right now. Don't wait another day to begin what you can start now.

CONTINUE TO THE FINISHING LINE

Successful people don't just start or do some initial work, they continue to work and do more until the barrier is totally removed and overpowered. Imagine a man that commenced a great project with pomp and excitement only to let go after the initial celebration. To him, it shall be reckoned as a failure.

Celebrate your milestones but do not stop until you have finished your entire project. There are times that people stop on the way to greater success because of small milestones along the way.

Starting is very important and needful but there is really no need to start if we do not make up our minds to continue to the end. Successful people have staying power. They are always determined not to give up along the way.

> And he sought to see who Jesus was, but could not because of the crowd, for he was of short stature. So he ran ahead and climbed up into a sycamore tree to see Him, for He was going to pass that way.
>
> *Luke 19:3 – 4 (NKJV)*

Sometimes, the fact that you have mastered your environment does not mean you have overcome your self-limitations. It is one thing to be free, it is another thing to be positioned for the blessing. This is the time for you to ARISE, ASCEND and MOVE UP to the heights that are above the norm! Zacheus was free from the crowd but was not yet well positioned for his dreams to come to pass. Instead of moaning and complaining of tiredness, he recognised that the job was not finished yet. He climbed up the sycamore tree so that he could see Jesus –

his intention was to fulfil his dreams. He distinguished himself, he overcame all the limitations and behold Jesus saw him and called him by name. There are times that people stop on the way to greater success because of small milestones along the way. Celebrate your milestones but do not stop until you have finished your entire project. If your goal is too small, make it bigger. You cannot afford to stop on the way. You must finish the work.

KEEP FOCUS

> Now Eliab his oldest brother heard when he spoke to the men; and Eliab's anger was aroused against David, and he said, "Why did you come down here? And with whom have you left those few sheep in the wilderness? I know your pride and the insolence of your heart, for you have come down to see the battle." And David said, "What have I done now? Is there not a cause?"
>
> *1 Samuel 17:28 – 29 (NKJV)*

David's brothers were his first detractors! Be careful who you listen to. There are people you should turn away from. David's brothers knew too much about him and so struggled to accept that he was able to achieve great things. You have to be careful of people who know too much about you especially if they are struggling to appreciate what you have been called to do. David remained, in the eyes of his brothers, a young lad who could not do anything. You have to learn to allow some people remain in your yesterday while you move on to your destiny.

You have to be careful of people who know too much about you especially if they are struggling to appreciate what you have been called to do.

As we have discussed earlier, do not allow what others think about you make you change the focus of your dreams. They had a negative opinion about him, but he had a positive opinion about himself. It is amazing that the people who doubt you are the ones you might expect to support you. Always remember that people fluctuate and that the information they have about you is not accurate. Stay away from negative and toxic associations. Successful people are aware that the people they surround themselves with will influence their decisions and consequently their outcomes. It is important to be deliberate about keeping your focus and setting your eyes in line with your agenda and purpose. You might not be able to convince everybody to see what you are seeing.

> But it so happened, when Sanballat heard that we were rebuilding the wall, that he was furious and very indignant, and mocked the Jews. And he spoke before his brethren and the army of Samaria, and said, "What are these feeble Jews doing? Will they fortify themselves? Will they offer sacrifices? Will they complete it in a day? Will they revive the stones from the heaps of rubbish— stones that are

burned?" Now Tobiah the Ammonite was beside him, and he said, "Whatever they build, if even a fox goes up on it, he will break down their stone wall."

Nehemiah 4:1 – 3 (NKJV)

There will always be Sanballats and Tobiahs. Don't pay attention to them. They are those who want to ridicule, distract, discourage, embarrass, harass and make you think you are too small to achieve the greatness that God is bringing you into. The danger is in listening to them. If you give yourself to what people say, you will lose the trust in your ability. They will make you feel sorry for yourself. If you listen too much to negative people, you will develop a complex about yourself because people are vicious. No man has enough information to determine your destiny.

If you listen too much to negative people, you will develop a complex about yourself because people are vicious.

You are heading for the presence of the king. Do not allow those who do not want to go anywhere stop you from reaching your goals.

BE COURAGEOUS

Courage is not the absence of fear. Courage is having strength to face your fears and to overcome when others are failing because of fear. Courage is an essential inner strength that is required for successful people if they want to stay on track without giving in. There will always be reasons to be afraid. Fear is not the problem, what you do about your fear is what matters.

> When Saul and all Israel heard these words of the Philistine, they were dismayed and greatly afraid.
>
> *1 Samuel 17:11 (NKJV)*

The children of Israel were incapacitated by the fear of Goliath. They could do nothing. They definitely desired the success, but their reactions to the fear that Goliath posed did not allow them to engage him in battle.

There will always be reasons to be afraid. Fear is not the problem, what you do about your fear is what matters.

Fear is one of the greatest limiters of destiny. If you give in to fear, you become incapacitated. Fearful people do not only lose their faith, they lose their mental and physical energy to achieve results. Fear is negative. Fear makes chickens of warriors and the valiant of men will tremble when they succumb to fear. Fear will make great warriors feeble!

David could have been scared like the rest of them, he could have considered the prowess and power of Goliath. Let's be sincere, no one would have blamed David if he pretended he was not paying attention to what Goliath was saying, after all it was not his business.

> Then David said to Saul, "Let no man's heart fail because of him; your servant will go and fight with this Philistine."
>
> *1 Samuel 17:32 (NKJV)*

David chose to pay attention to what Goliath was saying because he had a different spirit. He believed something could be done and he was ready to be the one who would shut this Goliath up on behalf of the armies of Israel. He was not going to allow fear to cripple his mind. Saul was a man of war who stayed away from the battle front because he also was afraid of Goliath. Fearful people around you can bring you into doubt if you do not deal with them rightly. Some of these fearful and doubting people might be sincere like Saul who was unable to do what David was intending to do but needed someone to take the shame away from Israel. Some others are mockers like the brothers of David because they did not believe that it was possible to achieve the kind of success David believed was possible.

Your success is not dependent on the circumstances or the people around you. You have to choose what you want.

All these doubters could have caused fear in David if he did not know how to deal with them. If you must be successful, it is expedient that you know how to deal wisely with the doubtful and the fearful. You must never allow them to win you to their side. You might not be able to get rid of them, just make sure you are not allowing them to get rid of your courage. Your success is not dependent on the circumstances or the people around you. You have to choose what you want.

REJECT EXCUSES

> The lazy man says, " There is a lion in the road! A fierce lion is in the streets!" As a door turns on its hinges, So does the lazy man on his bed. The lazy man buries his hand in the bowl; It wearies him to bring it back to his mouth. The lazy man is wiser in his own eyes than seven men who can answer sensibly.
>
> *Proverbs 26:13-16 (NKJV)*

It is amazing how this guy knew that a lion was outside on the road. All he was prepared to do was sleep and then sleep again. He needed an excuse to feed his failure. If you are looking for excuses, you will always find one. For you to continue in the face of excuses you must make a conscious effort to reject and refuse all excuses no matter how tenable they might look.

Interest will only carry you as long as the circumstances are favourable. Commitment will keep you on track irrespective of what you have to face.

Excuses are not reasons, they are makeshift positions that a lazy person occupies instead of stepping forward to face challenges in life. Nobody is successful because everything is in place. People are successful because they are ready to forge ahead even when the road seems unclear. There are so many contradictory situations and ideas in life that will stand against what you are planning to do in your journey of success. Sometimes you will never find the road until you have stepped out of your comfort zone into an area of seemingly impossible terrain.

Excuses are not reasons, they are makeshift positions that a lazy person occupies instead of stepping forward to face challenges in life.

Successful people are not just interested in pursuing their dreams, they are committed to it. Interest will only carry you as long as the circumstances are favourable. Commitment will keep you on track irrespective of what you have to face. With commitment, you are sold out, you are completely enraptured with the determination to get to your goals. Are you just interested or are you committed to moving on to success in life?

MASTER YOUR MISTAKES

Successful people do not back out of their purpose because of the mistakes of the past. Many people have been wounded and suffocated because of one or two mistakes they have made in business, in their leadership or in their life. Your mistakes are not as bad as you think they are. Don't be too hard on yourself. Let us be sincere, so many great people are products of mistakes. Do not be too careful to make mistakes. You do not want to be too paranoid that you end up not making any meaningful contribution to your own life. Remember, every mistake you make is another way not to do things and another pointer to the right direction. Those who live in fear of making mistakes are handicapped in their achievements.

Remember, every mistake you make is another way not to do things and another pointer to the right direction.

Inasmuch as we want to get decisions right, successful people understand that you learn from your mistakes and move further in life. Often times, it is arrogance that causes this fear to paralyse a lot of people in the pursuit of success. Do not be crippled by the fear of mistakes or even the mistakes you have made. You will always have another opportunity to do better. Go for your dreams!

CHAPTER SEVEN

THE FINAL WORD

God didn't make anyone to fail. We have all been fashioned by God to succeed in life. Our success story is therefore not a question of whether God wants us to prosper. The question is whether we really want to prosper and succeed in life.

The capacity to succeed is in every one of us but the reality of success is with only a few.

The capacity to succeed is in every one of us but the reality of success is with only a few. These few are those who are ready to believe that God wants success for them. These ones are willing to step into the journey of success with determination and unwavering commitment in spite of whatever hindrances may come their way.

SUCCESS LIES WITHIN YOU

How can you have hope in God and not believe that as long as you are joined to the living there is still hope? Many people are quick to write themselves off, walking away from that which they had trusted God for in their life. You are too anointed to give up. Don't let the devil cause you to let go of your destiny. You are fashioned by God to succeed! You must remain in hope to stay true to who you are. You are born to succeed.

Now Jabez was more honorable than his brothers, and his mother called his name Jabez, saying, "Because I bore him in pain." And Jabez called on the God of Israel saying, "Oh, that You would bless me indeed, and enlarge my territory, that Your hand would be with me, and that You would keep me from evil, that I may not cause pain!" So God granted him what he requested.

I Chronicles 4:9 – 10 (NKJV)

Jabez was given a bad name but he was not going to have it, he rejected it. He was not going to be limited by what others said. He turned to God and made a significant change in his life. Success is the best revenge. When people write you off, don't join them. Do not allow anyone tell you what God is not saying! What is the name they have given to you? What curse seems to be ruling your affairs? Who said you cannot make it? If you get alone with God, you will never be alone again! Take up this challenge and be ready to make something happen. The journey of a successful life begins when you begin to take the right actions in line with your purpose. Do not just make the decisions, start doing something about them right now. Remember, you have what it takes to succeed.

The journey of a successful life begins when you begin to take the right actions in line with your purpose.

I want to invite you into the journey of true success. Your success in life will only be defined by your purpose. Until we are in alignment with our purpose in life, all achievements are just mirages that will fade away with time. Genuine purpose in life begins with a realisation that we are here on earth for the sole purpose of fulfilling the will and plans of God for our lives. It is in this that our purpose is defined and through this we can connect to the true meaning of success. Success is not far from anyone who is interested in becoming all that God has destined them to be.

Your success in life will only be defined by your purpose.

Remember, God is always on your side. Start writing own your success story.